The Coloring Book of Vintage Inspired Flowers

An adult coloring book, Inspired by Vintage Illustrations of flowers!

Over 40 illustrations for hours of stress relieving fun!
This book makes a perfect gift for everyone!

Be sure to check us out on Facebook and our website for other great things!

http://breerspublishing.weebly.com/

https://www.facebook.com/BreersPublishing/

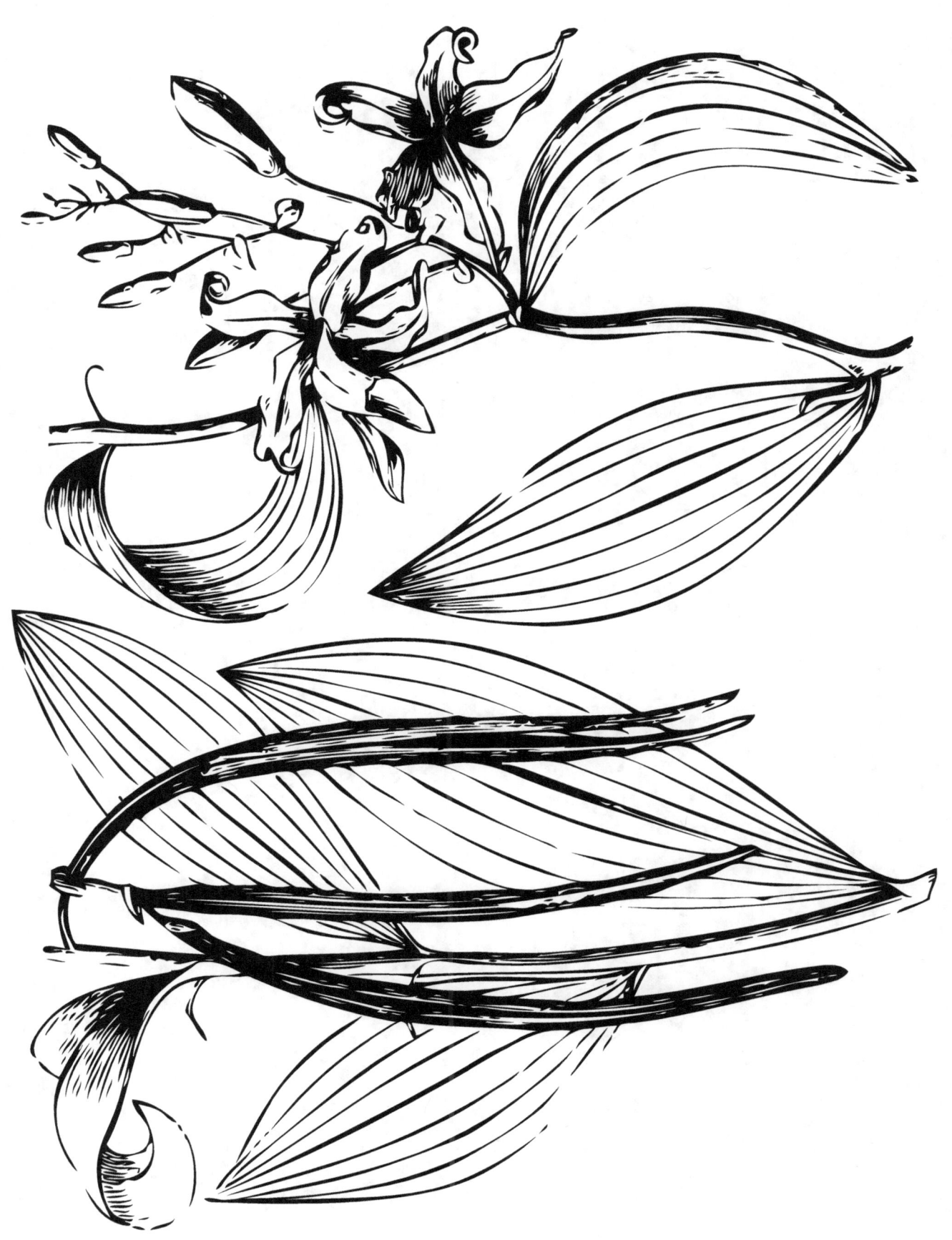

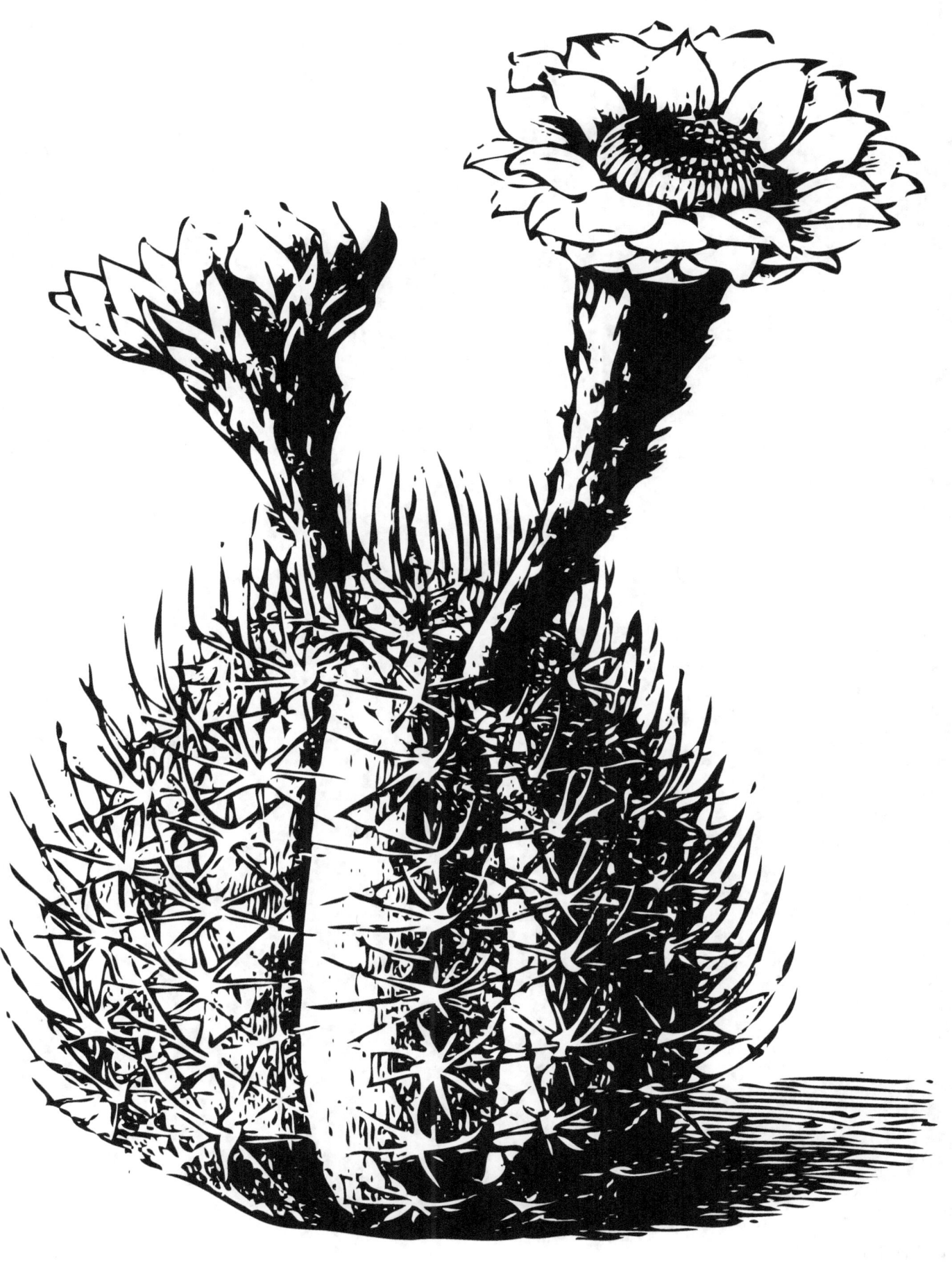